A HORRID FACTBOOK

HORRID HENRY'S
BODIES

Francesca Simon spent her
childhood on the beach in California, and
then went to Yale and Oxford Universities
to study medieval history and literature.
She now lives in London with her family.
She has written over fifty books and won the
Children's Book of the Year in 2008 at the
Galaxy British Book Awards for *Horrid Henry
and the Abominable Snowman*.

Tony Ross is one of Britain's
best-known illustrators, with many
picture books to his name as well as
line drawings for many fiction titles.
He lives in Oxfordshire.

Complete list of **Horrid Henry**
titles at the end of the book

Also by Francesca Simon

Don't Cook Cinderella
Helping Hercules

and for younger readers

Don't Be Horrid, Henry
Illustrated by Kevin McAleenan

The Topsy-Turvies
Illustrated by Emily Bolam

A HORRID FACTBOOK

HORRID HENRY'S BODIES

Francesca Simon
Illustrated by Tony Ross

Orion
Children's Books

First published in Great Britain in 2011
by Orion Children's Books
a division of the Orion Publishing Group Ltd
Orion House
5 Upper Saint Martin's Lane
London WC2H 9EA
An Hachette UK Company

3 5 7 9 10 8 6 4 2

Text © Francesca Simon 2011
Illustrations © Tony Ross 2011

Printed in Great Britain by
Clays Ltd, Elcograf S.p.A.

www.orionbooks.co.uk

www.horridhenry.co.uk

CONTENTS

Hello from Henry

Hold on tight, everyone, you are about to open the grisliest, grossest, most disgusting book ever! And it's all true, so your mean, horrible parents can't complain when you tell them all about bogies, earwax, mucus, wee or head lice. You name it, you'll find all the facts you need to know to gross out your teachers and revolt your friends. Yippee!

Henry

BLECCCH!
FOUL FACTS

The **loudest burp** recorded (so far) was 107.1 decibels – that's louder than the sound of a drill breaking up concrete!

When you sneeze, the air coming out of your nose and mouth travels at 100 miles per hour – even faster than cars on a motorway.

Did you know that you produce more than a litre of saliva every day?

Your nose also makes about a litre of **slimy glop** each day – called mucus. And most of it, you swallow. Eeew!

On a normal day, you produce about half a litre of sweat. But if it's hot and you do lots of exercise, you could produce up to seven litres. That's three and a half big bottles of fizzywizz!

The sweatiest part of your body isn't your armpits or your feet – it's the palms of your hands.

What's in a **bogey**? Dried mucus mixed with dust and dirt – with a few bugs to add extra flavour!

Can you believe it? You'll spend three years of your life on the toilet.

You produce about 45,000 litres of urine in a lifetime – enough to fill 450 baths.

Romans used to brush their teeth with urine. **Blecccch!**

Ever tried beetroot? If you eat too much of it, your wee will turn pink!

When an astronaut spacewalks on the moon, he wears something called a Maximum Absorption Garment. Sounds grand but it's really a **man-sized nappy**.

Long ago in the Fourteenth Century, it wasn't cool to wash, so people sprayed on lots of perfume to cover their **stinky smell** instead.

When you die, your skin shrinks and this makes your nails and hair look as though they're still growing. **Scary!**

Ancient Egyptians used to cut open a dead body, remove the insides and place them in a jar next to the coffin. Then they made a mummy by bandaging the body up in strips of linen.

Whenever you talk or chew, little clumps of **earwax** fall out of your ears. Luckily, they are too small to see.

INSIDE
INFO

If you could touch your brain, it would feel like **jelly**.

Just because your brain is small, doesn't mean you're not as clever as someone with a big brain.

Did you know that nearly two-thirds of your body is made up of water?

In your lifetime, your heart will beat about **2,500 million times** – and never take a rest.

Try clenching your fist – it's about the same size of your heart. As you get older and your fist grows bigger, so does your heart.

Your liver is the **largest** and **heaviest** organ inside your body, weighing an average of 1.6 kilograms. That's the same as three bags of pasta!

If your **blood vessels** were all stretched out like a piece of string, they would circle around the Earth twice.

It takes only one minute for a drop of blood to travel all around your body.

If you were ill in the Middle Ages, the doctor might have put **leeches** on your body to suck some of the blood out for you.

I wonder why they didn't try nits...

Our bodies are always 37°C – it doesn't matter if the weather's hot or cold. But cold–blooded animals like lizards have to warm themselves up in the sun.

Your smallest muscle is called the **stapedius** – it's in your ear and it helps to protect you from loud noises.

And your biggest muscle is in your bottom and is called the **gluteus maximus**.

There are more than **60 muscles** in your face – that's why you can make lots of funny expressions.

You use about **40 muscles to frown**, but only about 20 to smile. Being moody like Margaret must be very tiring!

Did you know you use 90 muscles in your leg every time you take a step?

Do you ever get **butterflies** in your tummy? If you're frightened or worried, the muscles in your tummy suddenly shorten and you get this funny fluttering feeling.

Ever put a shell to your ear and heard the sound of the sea? What you're really hearing are **sound waves** bouncing between the shell, your ear lobes, the inside of your ear and your eardrum.

If you took out your intestines and uncoiled them, they'd be about **four times** as tall as you.

Did you know that your stomach is full of strong acid that turns your food into liquid?

Just think how much is sloshing around in Greedy Graham's guts.

You breathe in and out about 15 times every minute – that's about 20,000 times a day.
Phew!

BRILLIANT
BONES

There are **206 bones** in an adult human skeleton.

As a newborn baby you have even more bones (up to 270) but many of them fuse together as you get older.

If you didn't have a skeleton, your body would collapse into a **shapeless lump**.

Did you know that your longest bone is in your thigh and is called the femur? It's roughly a quarter of your total height.

Can you bend any of your joints so far the wrong way that they look broken? If you can then you're **double-jointed**.

Your **smallest bone** is in your ear. It's called the stirrup bone and it's smaller than a grain of rice.

Measure your height in the morning and then again in the evening – you'll find you're smaller in the evening. This is the effect of **gravity** on your spine. Don't worry, during the night you'll go back to your full height again.

We all have 12 pairs of ribs, but about one person in five hundred has an extra one – lucky them!

Have you found your **funny bone**? It isn't really a bone – it's a nerve on your elbow. If you've ever banged it by mistake, you'll find that it isn't really funny either – it hurts!

In 3000 BC, doctors performed brain surgery on their patients by drilling a hole in their skulls – just to see what happened!

I wonder what you'd see if you drilled a hole in Margaret's skull...

SKIN, SCALES AND SCABS

Your skin is your heaviest and largest organ. An adult's skin weighs about four kilograms – the same weight as two big bottles of fizzywizz.

If a grown-up took off his skin and ironed it flat, it would be about the **size of a single bed**.

Your thinnest skin – 0.5mm – is on your eyelids.

Your thickest skin – 5mm thick and more – is on the soles of your feet.

Your skin might look and feel smooth, but really it's covered in lumps, bumps, ridges and grooves where **billions of body bugs** hide. Yeuch!

You've heard about snakes shedding their scaly skins – well, you do too! Every minute, about **50,000** tiny flakes of skin fall off your body.

Every month your body makes a new skin, and during your lifetime you'll have about 1,000 new skins.

If your dead skin cells didn't drop off, after three years your skin would be as thick as an **elephant's**.

When you cut yourself, your blood thickens to form a scab. The scab stops germs getting into the cut while your skin heals, so don't pick at it!

If you have a cut that's producing a thick yellow pus, act fast! It means that **germs** have got in, and your cut needs cleaning.

Do you like carrots?
Be careful, if you eat
too many of them, your
skin might **turn orange**.

If you ever need stitches, the doctor might use something called cat gut. But don't worry, it isn't really cat gut – it's made from sheep or goat intestines … so that's OK then!

HORRIBLY
HAIRY
FACTS

Did you know that you're just as hairy
as a gorilla? Luckily your body hair is much
shorter and thinner!

**Unless of course you're Bossy Bill or
Stuck-Up Steve.**

Have you noticed that you're hairy all over
apart from a few places? Only the soles of
your feet and the palms of your hands are
hair-free.

About 100 hairs fall out of your head every
day. But don't worry, new ones grow to
replace them all the time!

**Too bad that's not true for Mr Mossy.
Tee hee.**

Your hair and nails might look and feel very different, but they're made of the same stuff – something called **keratin**.

Hair grows faster at night and also faster in the summer – strange but true!

Ever wondered what your eyebrows are for? They help stop sweat dropping into your eyes.

Eyebrows show people how you're feeling. If you raise them you look surprised, if you lower them, you look puzzled, and if you lower them right down, you look angry.

Mum and Dad have lowered eyebrows all the time.

When you're cold, you get **goose pimples** and your body hairs stand on end. This traps air and helps keep your body warm.

Your hair stands on end when you're frightened. In Prehistoric times, this **hair-raising effect** was supposed to make us look bigger to frighten our enemies.

Men have more nose hair than women ... and it grows longer and longer as they get older.

Wow! A woman in China grew her hair to 5.6 metres – the longest ever recorded. If she leaned out of a window on the second floor of a house, her hair would touch the ground.

The **longest beard** ever measured was only
a little bit shorter than the record-breaking
hair, at 5.33 metres long.

An Indian man grew the
longest ear hair ever –
18.1cm. It sprouted out of
the middle of his ears, and
hung right down to his
shoulders.

When Elizabeth I was Queen of England,
it was the fashion for ladies to pluck out
some of their hair to make their foreheads
look very high.

I bet you didn't know that whales have hair too – not very much though.

If you're fair-haired you have about **130,000 hairs** on your head – quite a lot more than your brown, black or red-haired friends.

Do you ever brush your hair? In Victorian times, you'd have been told to brush it a hundred times a day.

Boring. I'm glad I'm not a Victorian.

EYES
IN-DEPTH

Around **80%** of people have brown eyes.
The rest have blue, green, hazel or grey eyes.

Most babies are born with blue eyes, but
not many stay blue. Most of them change
to brown, hazel, grey or green.

Your pupils, the black spots in the centre
of your eyes, are really holes that let in light,
which is why they get bigger in the dark and
smaller in the bright sunshine.

If you see someone you like, your heart beats
faster and this makes your pupils get bigger too.

Cats can see better than humans in the dark because their pupils let in more light, and they also use their whiskers to find their way about.

Unless of course your cat is like Fat Fluffy, who never moves.

Owls can see well at night too because they have very big pupils.

Owls can't move their eyes like we can. They can move their whole heads almost right round instead.

Rabbits and parrots can see behind themselves without turning their heads.

Squids have the largest eyes. They are 25cm across – as large as a dinner plate.

In your lifetime, you will blink **415 million times**.

If you live to 75, you'll have cried 12 buckets worth of tears.

Lots of animals cry tears when they're in pain, but only humans cry tears when they are upset.

Even Weepy William would find it impossible to cry in space – **no gravity** means your tears won't trickle.

Gorgeous Gurinder's long eyelashes are very good at doing their job – stopping dust, dirt and insects from getting in her eyes.

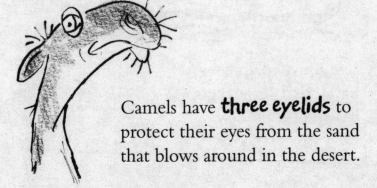

Camels have **three eyelids** to protect their eyes from the sand that blows around in the desert.

Did you know that strong
sunshine can damage your
eyes? You should always wear
sunglasses and never look
directly at the sun.

Even when a snake has its eyes closed,
it can still see through its eyelids. **Sneaky!**

TERRIBLE TONGUES

The average length of a human tongue is 10cm from the back of the throat to the tip of the tongue.

A giraffe has such a long tongue – 53cm – that it can **clean its own ears**.

A blue whale's tongue weighs more than an elephant and **50 humans** could stand on it.

Crocodiles can't move their tongues and they can't chew – but they can swallow . . .

A chameleon's tongue is nearly twice the length of its body. It shoots in and out to catch insects so fast that we can't see it happen.

Snakes smell with their tongues. When they flick their tongues in and out, they are sniffing out food and danger.

A giraffe's tongue is **bluish-black** in colour – to stop it getting sunburned while the giraffe eats.

Your tongue has about 10,000 tiny taste buds, but they are so small you can't see them.

Over the years, some taste buds die and are not replaced. So kids have the best taste buds.

No wonder Mum and Dad like sprouts so much!

When you're really old, you might catch an infection called **black hairy tongue**. Your taste buds swell up and go a funny colour, and your tongue looks dark and furry.

Or you could be Margaret and have it now.

HANDY
FACTS

Your **fingerprints** are formed when you're just three months old inside your mum's tummy.

Your fingerprints are completely unique. Even identical twins have different prints.

One person in ten is left-handed, and boys are more likely to be left-handed than girls.

If you're left-handed, the nails on your left hand grow faster than the ones on your right.

And if you're right-handed, the nails on your right hand grow faster than those on your left.

Some people can write just as well with both their hands – this is called being **ambidextrous**.

Most nails grow 0.5 millimetres each week.

Some people never cut their nails – and nails have been known to grow up to 90cm long.

If you bite your nails – be warned! There are more germs under your fingernails than **under the toilet seat**.

SUPER
SENSES

We have **five senses** – touch, taste, sight, smell and hearing.

Your senses of smell and taste work together. If something smells bad, you won't like the taste of it – this stops you eating mouldy or poisonous food.

Some people have **synaesthesia**, which means their senses are mixed up. They hear colours, feel sights and smell tastes.

If you're colour-blind, you can't tell the difference between red and green.

More boys than girls are colour-blind.

Some people suffer from total colour blindness and see everything in shades of grey – like an old black-and-white film.

Most mammals see the world in **black** and **white**.

Moles live underground, and they have poor eyesight, so they use touch and smell to find their food.

Did you know that your nose can remember more than **10,000 different smells**?

Your sense of touch is felt by your nerve-endings, particularly on your tongue, lips and fingertips.

Bats use sound to see in the dark. When they squeak, the sound waves hit whatever's in front of them, and bounce back to their ears like **an echo**.

Your taste buds recognise four basic tastes: salty, sweet, bitter (like coffee) and sour (like lemons).

Have you heard of **ultrasound**? Some animals, like dogs, cats, dolphins, bats and mice can hear ultrasound, but it's too high for human ears.

SNOOZE
NEWS

You're probably going to spend about one-third of your life asleep.

Lazy Linda spends about two-thirds of hers asleep!

The average person falls asleep in **seven minutes**.

Getting lots of sleep helps you grow.

Your brain needs to rest too – which is why if you don't get enough sleep, you'll get **very moody**!

A newborn baby sleeps for 20 hours a day, while a ten year old sleeps for around ten hours.

Just like Lazy Linda, some animals love to sleep. Pythons sleep for 18 hours a day, tigers for 16 and cats for 12.

Fat Fluffy sleeps 24 hours a day.

Snails sometimes sleep for three years.

Every year, you have about 1,000 dreams. Most of them, you'll forget.

Cows can sleep standing up, but they can only dream lying down.

The **loudest snore** ever recorded was 93 decibels – that's louder than the sound of the traffic on the motorway!

That's almost how loud New Nick snored when I had a sleepover at his house.

The current record for going without sleep is 11 days. **Yawn!**

AMAZING
ANIMALS

There are **100,000 muscles** in an elephant's trunk, while you have only 650 skeletal muscles in your whole body.

Under all their fluffy white fur, polar bears actually have black skin.

Most tigers have more than 100 stripes, and every tiger has a different pattern.

If you shaved off a tiger's stripy fur, you'd discover that it has **stripy skin** too.

Flamingos are born grey and white – it's all
the shrimp they eat that turns them pink.

A hippopotamus can open its mouth
1.2 metres wide – just about enough to
fit in a ten-year-old boy or girl.

**I wonder if I could trick Stuck-Up Steve
or Moody Margaret into going near one?**

The **most venomous** spider
in the world is the Brazilian
Wandering Spider – just
the tiniest drop of its
venom can kill a mouse.

Skunks defend themselves with stinky spray,
so don't get too close!

Cobras protect themselves by shooting poison into their enemies' eyes and blinding them for a while. It's very painful too!

To scare off enemies, the horned lizard **squirts blood** from its eyelids.

That's brilliant. Wish I could.

The only bird that can **fly backwards** is the hummingbird.

Bats are the only mammals that can fly.

The largest frog is about 30cm long, and the smallest is less than 2cm.

Frogs don't drink water – they absorb it through their skin.

Shrews eat their own **body weight** in food every day.

Even Greedy Graham can't do that, though he tries . . .

An ostrich egg weighs well over a kilo – it would take 40 minutes to hard-boil it.

The Ancient Greeks used to blow up a **pig's bladder** and play football with it.

A rhinoceros's horn might look as though it's made of bone, but it's actually made out of hair.

DEEP-SEA
DATA

A blue whale's heart is the size of a small car.

If a shark is charging at you, it can't stop – it can only swerve to one side.

Sharks can't swim backwards.

The largest jellyfish ever found was 2.3 metres long – even longer than your bed.

Sharks can **smell blood** in the water up to five kilometres away.

The blue whale can make an ear-splitting 188 decibel sound. That's nearly twice as loud as a road drill and it can be heard underwater over 800 kilometres away.

When a puffer fish is scared, it swallows water or air and blows itself up into a big, spiny ball.

If a shark stops beating its tail, it will sink.

An octopus has three hearts.

If a starfish loses an arm, it can grow another one.

Emperor penguins can stay under water for an amazing **11 minutes**. The human record for staying underwater is 7.5 minutes – which is also very impressive.

Sometimes sharks go to sleep at night on the sea floor. **Aah!**

CRAZY CREEPY-CRAWLIES

Bedbugs hate the sunshine, so they come out and bite you at night.

Head lice love **sucking blood** from your scalp. But don't panic, they're so tiny you won't feel a thing.

Sometimes head lice are so greedy that they drink too much of your blood, their stomachs spring a leak and they die. What a shame!

Female head lice glue their eggs to your hair using a special super-strong glue. Even if you wash your hair or go swimming, those eggs will stay stuck!

A broad tapeworm can grow inside your intestine for years, reaching a length of ten metres. **Aaagh!**

Buzzy insects like bees don't make noises with their voices – but by moving their wings very quickly.

A leech will gorge itself on blood until it is **five times bigger** than when it started.

A caterpillar has more muscles in its body than Aerobic Al (or anyone else!).

Cockroaches can flatten themselves and slide into tiny cracks in the wall.

A slug can stretch itself out about **twenty times** its normal length, and then squeeze into tight spaces.

Butterflies taste with their feet.

An ant can lift **ten times** its own body weight.

When you feel an itch, you scratch it because your brain thinks it might be an insect trying to suck your blood.

The greatest number of **bee stings** ever survived is 2,243. Ouch!

Spiders have **48 knees** – eight legs with six joints on each.

BIGGEST, SMALLEST, FASTEST, TALLEST . . .

Biggest overall – the blue whale is the largest living mammal at up to 34 metres long – that's the length of four double-decker buses – and 150 tonnes – that's more than the weight of 21 elephants.

Biggest land animal – the African bush elephant, weighing nearly seven tonnes.

Tallest land animal – the giraffe, which can be over six metres tall – as tall as your house.

Tallest known human was 2.73 metres tall. If you sit on your dad's shoulders you'll get some idea how big that is.

Smallest mammal – pygmy shrews, weighing less than six grams, the same as a 50p piece.

Smallest bird – the hummingbird weighs 28 grams – even less than a small bag of crisps.

Smallest known human was 56cm small – just up to the third step of a staircase, or the length of a junior tennis racquet.

Fattest animals – ringed seal pups. Half of their body is fat!

Fattest known human was 636 kilograms – that's approximately 18 tubby two-week-old seal pups!

Fastest animal – the cheetah, running at speeds of up to 100 kilometres per hour. Ask your mum or dad to tell you when they're driving at around 60 miles an hour – that's how fast the cheetah can run!

Fastest human ran at 37.3 kilometres per hour. This is around your driving speed in a 20 miles per hour zone – feels slow in the car, but it's fast on foot.

Fastest swimmer – the dolphin – at 56 kilometres per hour – that's nearly 19 lengths in a minute.

That's almost as fast as I can swim. Just ask Soggy Sid if you don't believe me.

Fastest bird – the peregrine falcon, which dives on a victim at 290 kilometres per hour, that's as fast as a high-speed train.

Slowest animal – the sloth, which moves at only two kilometres per hour – that's like you walking really slowly.

Highest jumper – kangaroos can jump over three metres high. They can jump over an elephant!

Highest human jump is 2.45 metres high, only a bit lower than the record-breaking kangaroo.

Deepest diver – the Antarctic penguin, diving to depths of 400 metres, almost the length of three and a half football pitches.

Brainiest mammal – human beings.

Brainiest bird – the hummingbird has the largest brain, which is nearly half of its total body weight.

Longest life – Asian elephants live nearly as long as humans, with the oldest one ever living to 78.

Longest human life – 122 years and 164 days.

Largest ears – the African elephant at 2 × 1.5 metres, about the size of a sheet for a double bed.

GROWING
PAINS

Between the ages of 6 and 12, you might feel pain in your legs during the night. Don't worry, it just means you're growing taller very fast!

When you're a teenager, you'll really spurt up in height, sometimes growing up to **9cm a year**.

Your brain stops growing when you are 15 years old.

But I think Peter's stopped growing ages ago.

Babies have **really big heads**! About a quarter of a baby's height is its head, but grown-ups' heads are only an eighth of their height.

 Ask your mum what time you were born. More babies are born between three and four o'clock in the morning than at any other hour.

Your **nose** and **ears** continue growing throughout your entire life!

Five hundred years ago, not many people lived past the age of 50…

… and not many men grew to more than 1.55 metres tall either, the same height as an average 12-year-old boy today.

Your eyes stay the same size throughout your life, which is why babies have such big eyes.

CAN YOU
DO
THIS . . . ?

Can you roll up your tongue? If you can, you're not alone – 85% of the population can do it too.

Can you sneeze with your eyes open? It's impossible!

Try eating a **sugary doughnut** without licking your lips. It's difficult because your body's natural instinct is to clean up the mess.

Can you eat more than three cream crackers in a row? You won't be able to because your mouth can't produce enough **saliva** to cope with them.

It's impossible to lick your own elbow –
unless you're very **double-jointed**.
(I bet you just tried it, didn't you?)

Can you pat your head
with one hand and
rub your tummy
at the same time?
Go on – try it!

Sit down, lift your right foot off the floor and make circles with it in a clockwise direction. At the same time, try drawing a number 6. Can you do it?

Can you stand on one leg, arms at your sides, with your eyes closed? You'll be **wobbly** because your balance is affected by your eyesight.

Are you ticklish? If you're happy, being tickled makes you laugh. But if you're feeling worried or sad, you might get upset if someone tickles you.

Have you ever had **pins and needles**? You can get this if you sit in a funny position and squash a nerve.

Try bending your wrist as far as it will go, then clench your fist and see what happens. One of your muscles is overpowering the other.

Rotate the fingers of both your hands in a clockwise direction. Go faster and faster and soon you'll find that your fingers are going in opposite directions.

When you're with a friend, do a big yawn. Your friend will yawn too, because **yawning is infectious**!

Can you juggle with three balls? If you can, that's brilliant but you'll have to beat 12 balls to win the world record.

How long can you stand on one foot? The world record is 76 hours and 40 minutes!

Do you ever get hiccups? The longest anyone has had hiccups is 69 years!

How do you feel when you've had the giggles? You should feel better, because laughter relaxes your body and is very good for you.

Can you touch your nose or chin with your tongue? Not many people can!

Can you raise one eyebrow, or twitch your nose, or wiggle your ears? If you can, you're very good at controlling your muscles.

Can you say this **tongue twister** fast five times:

If a black bug bleeds black blood,
what colour blood does a blue bug bleed?

Tricky? That's because it's difficult for your brain and tongue to work together.

Bye!

HORRID HENRY BOOKS

Colour Books

Horrid Henry's Big Bad Book
Horrid Henry's Wicked Ways
Horrid Henry's Evil Enemies
Horrid Henry Rules the World
Horrid Henry's House of Horrors
Horrid Henry's Dreadful Deeds
Horrid Henry Shows Who's Boss

Joke Books

Horrid Henry's Joke Book
Horrid Henry's Jolly Joke Book
Horrid Henry's Might Joke Book
Horrid Henry versus Moody Margaret
Horrid Henry's Hilariously Horrid Joke Book

Activity Books

Horrid Henry's Brainbusters
Horrid Henry's Headscratchers
Horrid Henry's Mindbenders
Horrid Henry's Colouring Book
Horrid Henry's Puzzle Book
Horrid Henry's Sticker Book
Horrid Henry's Classroom Chaos
Horrid Henry's Holiday Havoc
Horrid Henry Runs Riot
Horrid Henry's Annual 2011

Visit Horrid Henry's website at
www.horridhenry.co.uk
for competitions, games, downloads and a monthly newsletter.